Holly's Walks

Walks for dogs (and people) in the Wye Valley

Philip Charlesworth

Second Edition

To the wonderful ladies in my life.
Holly, my dog, and Ruth, my wife.

This book would not have been possible without some help. Several dogs and their people have acted as guinea pigs for testing the routes. Particular thanks go to Pongo and his human Rosie, Harley with her human Naya, Casper, Bramble and Benson with their human Kate, Harvey and his human Richie, and Cassie with her human Helen.

Holly

Pongo

Harley

Benson

Casper

Bramble

Harvey

Cassie

The Editorial Panel

The front cover photo is Holly in the River Wye near Symonds Yat. The rear cover picture was taken at Little Doward.

Key to Maps

Main road

Minor road

Track suitable for vehicles

Footpath, Bridleway

Cycle route

WVW *Wye Valley Walk*

ODP *Offa's Dyke Path*

Lake. stream

Woods

Cliffs

Buildings

P *Car park*

Caves, mines

Trig point

FB *Footbridge*

1 *Waypoint*

Campsite

Gate, Barrier

Mast

Other feature

Viewpoint

Picnic area

Bridge

Contents

Introduction

The Second Edition

The first edition of this book was a labour of love for Holly and her Labrador friends. It was quite a pleasant surprise to find that other dog walkers shared our love of this beautiful area and bought copies of the book. Thank you all. It led to a sequel which described our favourite walks in the Forest of Dean which has become equally popular.

Walks in this book all lie within the Wye Valley Area of Outstanding Natural Beauty (AONB), and have been selected for their quality and interest. In addition to is spectacular beauty, the AONB has many different habitats and supports a wide range of wildlife.

Since writing the first edition there have been many small changes to the walks so the maps and directions needed to be updated. One walk has been made unsightly by extensive forestry work and has been removed from the book. The creation of new car parks has opened up some new areas, adding three new walks to the book.

Holly and I hope that you find these walks as enjoyable as we do.

The Walks

The Wye Valley AONB straddles the border between England and Wales. The AONB contains many areas of access woodland and an extensive network of tracks and paths. Three national trails go through the area: Offa's Dyke Path, the Wye Valley Walk and the Wysis Way. It includes breathtaking scenery, spectacular viewpoints and diverse wildlife. It's easy to see why this area is so popular with walkers.

This book includes our favourite walks from around the AONB. Finding walks that included good scenery and viewpoints is easy in an AONB, but dog walkers need more than just good scenery. We need large areas where we can let our dogs off lead. We need to know that there are no awkward stiles; Lifting a 27kg Labrador over a stile is not easy! Its nice to have dog friendly pubs and cafes so we can rest our legs. We need to know where there are poop bins. All these things have been considered while writing this book.

The walks in this book vary from 1.6km to 12.8 km in length and

The view from Symonds Yat

are located in the southern Wye Valley between Chepstow and Symonds Yat. Pages 6 and 7 show locations of these walks on maps of the area. The walks have been graded as easy, moderate and hard.

Easy The walk follows good tracks and paths. There are a few small slopes but no big hills.

Moderate The walk is mainly on good tracks and paths but some uneven ground will be encountered. There are a few significant hills.

Hard The walk is quite long and includes some rough ground and long, steep, hills.

The walks can be accessed from the main routes through the area. The A40 is a dual carriageway that links Abergavenny and the bottom of the M50 at Ross-on-Wye. A466 follows the valley bottom from the M48 J2 at Chepstow to Monmouth, passing through Tintern and Llandogo. The 4293 takes the high ground to the west of the valley, going from Chepstow to Monmouth, passing through Devauden and Trellech. Directions to the walks originate from these roads. In between the A466 and B4293 are numerous small lanes that serve the farms and villages. One of these lanes goes from Trellech to the Wye Valley Hotel at Tintern, giving access to Beacon Hill (chapter 5), Ninewells Wood (chapter 6) and Bargain Wood (chapter 7).

Wildlife

The Wye Valley has many different habitats, and a wide variety of wildlife to match. The rivers and ponds, extensive woods, heathland, cliffs and fields supports many species of birds and mammals.

Fallow Deer can be seen throughout the valley, especially the woodland areas. During early morning or late evening walks it is common to see them disappearing into the trees as you approach. Roe Deer and Muntjac Deer are less common but we've seen both on late evening walks in the summer.

Wild boar from the Forest of Dean have started to enter the Wye Valley. Signs of boar are common on the eastern side of the river between Symonds Yat and Staunton and are starting to appear on the Western side. At the time of writing boar have been confirmed in the woods between Chepstow and Tintern, including Chepstow Park Wood. Boar are generally timid and will avoid contact if possible, preferring to stay deep in the woods away from people. They can be dangerous when protecting young piglets, especially if surprised. In the unlikely event that you encounter a boar put your dog on its lead and walk away.

Otters have established a presence on the Wye. While rarely seen, the population is reported to be healthy and growing. Bats, too, have established themselves around the whole valley, taking advantage of stone barns and limestone caves.

The Wye Valley is a great place for birdwatchers. During our walks we often see buzzards patrolling the edge of the woods and, less frequently, Sparrowhawks. Peregrine Falcon nests can be seen at Symonds Yat from the viewing platform, and they can occasionally be seen hunting around the valley edge. Woodland birds such as long-tailed tits, blackcaps and nuthatches are very common in the woodland around the valley. Waterbirds such as swans, ducks and herons are a common sight when walking the riverbanks.

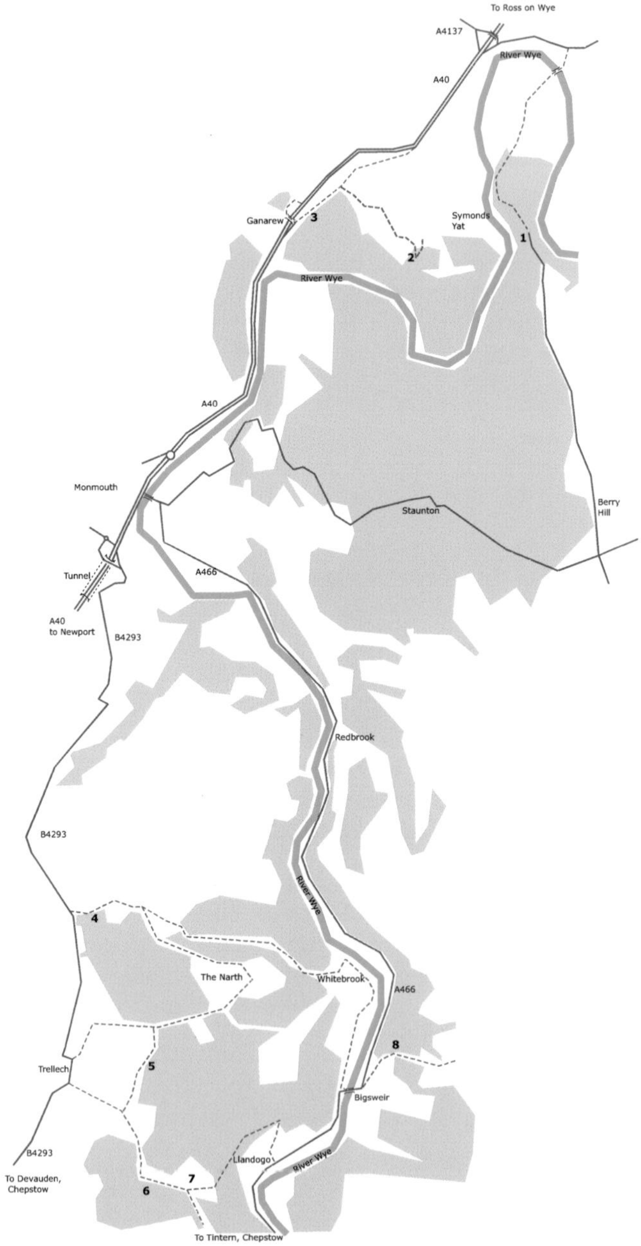

Locations of the Walks - Map 1

Locations of the Walks - Map 2

What to Take

Every dog owner understands the importance of a good waterproof jacket for those days when its tipping down with rain and the dog has to be walked. Some of these paths are rough underfoot so good footwear is important, especially on long or hard walks. Most of the year I find that walking boots are perfectly satisfactory around the valley. In winter, or after protracted periods of rain, Wellingtons are advisable as some of the paths get muddy. I've highlighted in the text if there are any particular sections that are bad after rain.

Ordnance Survey maps were used a lot when planning the walks. It quickly became clear that there are several forest trails marked on OS maps that don't appear on the ground, possibly because they have fallen into disuse and have become overgrown. Other paths do not appear on the OS maps, for example new paths created during forestry works. The maps in this book show the paths that actually exist and have not changed over the last few years.

The Wye Valley is very deep, 400ft in places, and the woodland is quite dense in places. Mobile phone signals are not always reliable so its prudent to think about what you would do in an emergency. I carry a small human/dog first aid kit in my bag, and a mobile phone just in case there is a signal. There are vets in Chepstow and Monmouth, and its prudent to know where they are and carry their phone numbers.

The custom in this area is to bag and remove all poop from public areas and popular tracks. Please don't hang bags from trees or throw them into the undergrowth; take them home with you. On quieter paths find a loose stick and flick poops into the undergrowth.

And remember to carry a camera, with spare batteries, because this area is beautiful!

And Finally...

We hope that you enjoy our choice of walks through this beautiful area. If, on your walks, you see a yellow Labrador with a bespectacled and slightly overweight man then it might be us. Please stop and chat.

Geology of the Wye Valley

These are the main rocks of the area, starting with the topmost and ending with the bedrock. The Wye cut through these rock layers over the last 2 million years to form the gorge.

Oolitic limestone. A generally rough surface as it shatters more easily than Dolostone. Formed 345-347 million years ago.

Dolostone. A hard magnesium-rich limestone, with a hard and smooth appearance. Formed 345-359 million years ago.

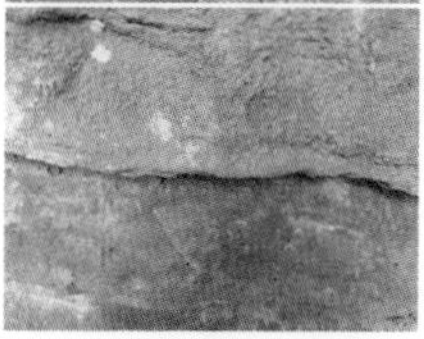

Tintern Sandstone. Can have a yellowish or reddish appearance. Formed 347-372 million years ago.

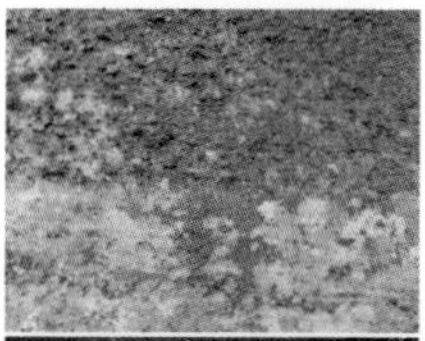

Quartz Conglomerate, locally known as pudding stone. Sandstone with embedded quartz pebbles. Formed 359-372 million years ago.

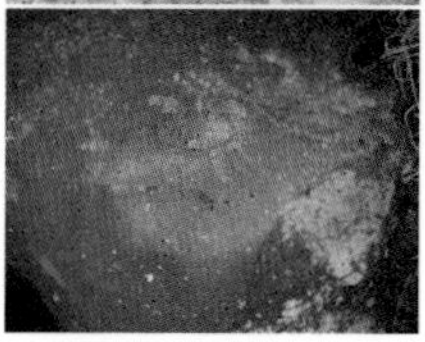

Old Red Sandstone. The foundation rock for the whole region. Formed 393-419 million years ago.

Symonds Yat

Short Route
Distance : 6.1km
Difficulty : Moderate

Long Route
Distance : 12.8km
Difficulty : Hard

Walk Description

This chapter offer two walks. The short route gives a sample of the area with a walk along the river and back through the woods. The long route includes many of the natural and man-made features of this stretch of the valley, for example the Suck Stone, Biblin's Bridge and the Near Hearkening Rocks. It incorporates some great scenery including an extended walk along the riverbank.

Both routes start and finish at Symonds Yat. A visit to Symonds Yat must include a trip to the viewpoint, with its views over the valley and bird-of-prey nests.

The routes have been chosen so that most of the uphill sections are not too steep, in fact there are only three short steep sections along the long route, the longest of which is only 150m. A fair level of fitness is required, and comfortable walking boots are recommended for the long route as some of the paths are uneven.

How to get there

Starting from the Wye Bridge in Monmouth, cross the bridge and go straight across the mini-roundabouts beside LIDL and the Mayhill Hotel. Follow the A 4136 for 5 miles as it winds its way up to the Forest of Dean plateau.

Take the left turn signposted for Symonds Yat and English Bicknor. Follow this road for about half a mile, then fork left following the brown tourist signs for Symonds Yat Rock. The entrance to the Symonds Yat Rock car park is about one mile from the fork on the left.

Car parking costs were £5.00 all day in 2020 with discounted

Playing in the River

prices in winter. The pay machine for the car park, and the poop bin, are just outside the toilet block. You can also leave poop bags in the general waste bins by the cafe.

Directions Starting at the car park, head for the toilet block. After paying for your parking take the path that passes the toilet block and follow it to the Log Cabin cafe.
There is a picnic area beside the cafe. At the back left corner of the picnic area there is a way post that marks the top of a flight of uneven stone steps. Take these steps, noting that they open up to the road in two places so keep your dog on its lead. The point at which a path crosses the bottom of the steps is point ❶. Turn sharp left onto a path that slopes down across the hillside behind the cafe. This path heads down to the river. As you follow it you might hear the calls of rock climbers on the crags higher up the slope. At one point you pass a substantial steel mesh that is intended to stop rocks from rolling onto the buildings below.
As you go down the path you'll become aware of the sound of the river passing over some small rapids, and catch a few glimpses of the river through the trees. At the bottom of the path (point ❷)

Biblins Bridge

you'll be on a pair of parallel tracks with the river on your right. Go to the river and head downstream.

For a while there is a footpath between these tracks and the water. There are several places where you can get access to the river and, if the current not too strong, it's a nice place for dog to have a paddle on a hot day. In autumn there are blackberry bushes along the river bank.

After a long straight stretch the track starts to bend to the right. You'll reach a track junction with a wooden sign saying "Symonds Yat East $1\frac{1}{4}$ miles" and "Biblins Bridge $\frac{1}{4}$ mile". This is point ❸ where the short walk and the long walk separate.

The Short Walk

Leave the river, and turn left onto the track that gently climbs into the woods. Initially this track takes you through a craggy valley with moss covered boulders. After a while it widens into open woodland. There is a little stream on your left that offers dogs another opportunity to cool off on a hot day.

After 1km you'll reach point ❾, where big track joins from the left. There is a sign pointing back to the river Wye. Turn left onto this track and follow it for about 2km until you reach a barrier. This is the exit road for the car park. Turn left, and follow the verge back to the car park and the start.

The Suckstone

The Long Walk Continue along the river to Biblins Bridge, point ❹. You have just left England and enter Wales. When you get to Biblins Bridge take some time to look at this amazing structure. First built in 1957, it was refurbished in the 1990s, badly damaged by floods in 2020 and is still in continuous use. It has wire mesh sides so its safe for dogs, and has lovely views up and down river from the middle of the bridge. Be aware that it is designed to only take 6 people at a time.

Follow the track past Biblins Bridge and continue along the river. The track passes under some overgrown cliffs on the left before reaching a small bench on the right. For the next few hundred meters there are several small paths that lead to the waters edge. It's worth exploring these as they lead to some beautiful views of the river.

Continuing along the track you come to the remains of an old limestone quarry on the left. Limestone was quarried in this area for many years for use in agriculture and building, but most of the quarries along the valley close during the late 19th century. The quarry is now overgrown, but the ruins of the old buildings and retaining walls are still visible.

After 1.5km you'll see a gravel island appear in the middle of the river. At the far end of the island the track narrows between two rocks, and a track comes in from the left. This is point ❺.

Turn left onto the track, which curves back to the left then turns sharp right to a green iron gate. After the gate the track slowly ascends with fields on the right and, eventually, a deer fence on the left. Looking across the fields you can see the steeple of St Mary's Church in Monmouth.

Keep following the deer fence when the path forks left. Follow the path as it steepens for about 100m before you come to a wide track. Turn right along the track for about 500m. As you come around a left hand bend look for a waypost and four steps on the left. This is point ❻. Go up the steps and a short path leads you to the Suckstone. You can't miss it - it weighs 30,000 tons! The Suckstone and the cliffs above it are formed of a sandstone and quartz agglomerate.

At the far end of the Suckstone a small path goes into the undergrowth. After about 50m the path reaches another waypost. Turn left, straight up the hill, and you reach the Near Hearkening Rocks. These overhanging cliffs were reputedly a favourite spot for gamekeepers as the curve of the rocks would focus the sounds of the poachers in the woods below. They are also a nice sheltered spot for a rest.

You don't need to climb the cliffs, although people have tried. There is a path at the left end of the cliffs that zigzags around them, leading to an obvious path that leads away from the cliff-top. As you walk away from the cliffs through the woods you come to a track and a waypost. Turn left onto the track and follow it as it gently curves to the right.

As you complete the long bend you come to the fence of Lady Park Wood, and re-enter England. Follow the fence, keeping it on your left. At the end of the fence turn left for a 500m descent on a small path to point ❼. This is rough in places so watch your footing.

As you go downhill another path crosses you at the Lady Park Wood sign. Ignore it and continue straight down the hill on the small path.

At the bottom of the hill you reach a track. This is point ❼.There is a waypost that is covered with direction signs. Go straight across the track onto a path that trends leftwards across the hill side

After a short steep climb (the last on this walk) the path levels a bit, then contours rightwards around the end of the hill. About 600m along the path you pass a short section of wooden handrail. After this handrail the path goes uphill for a short distance to a fork, marked with a waypost. Take the left fork and head downhill for 250m to the track at point ❽.

Allow time for a refreshment stop at the Log Cabin

Turn right along the track. There is a little stream on your left that offers dogs another opportunity to cool off on a hot day.
After a while you'll reach point ❾, where big track joins from the left. There is a sign pointing back to the river Wye. Turn left onto this track and follow it for about 2km until you reach a barrier. This is the exit road for the car park. Turn left, and follow the verge back to the car park and the start.
We have a tradition that, after the walk, Holly and I go to the Log Cabin for a coffee and flapjack.

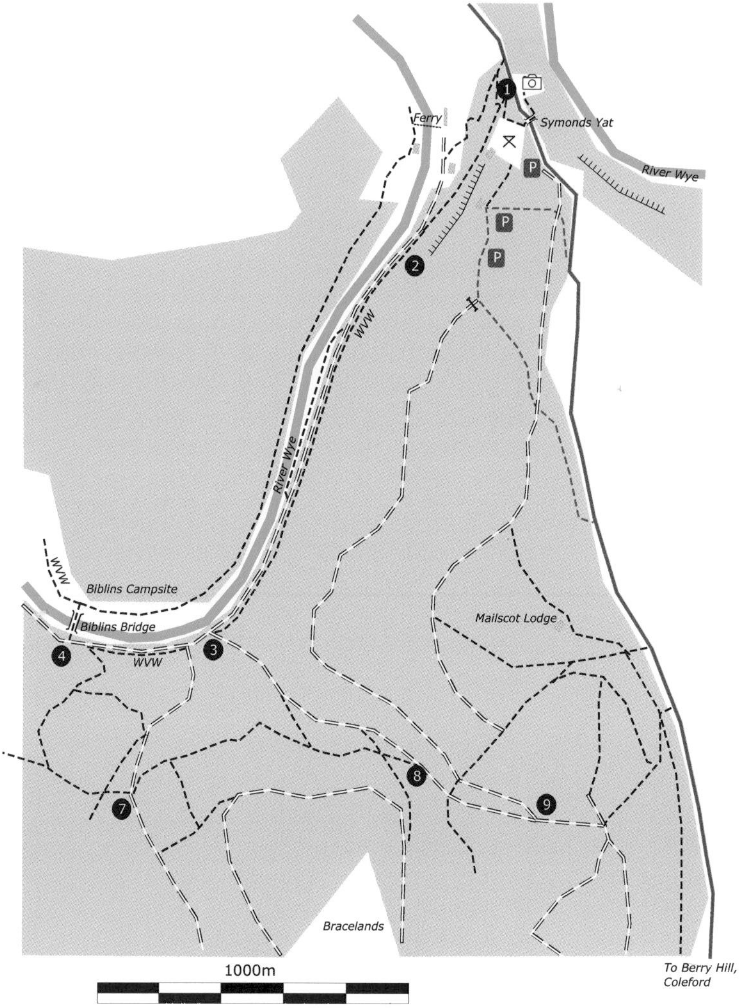

Symonds Yat Map 1

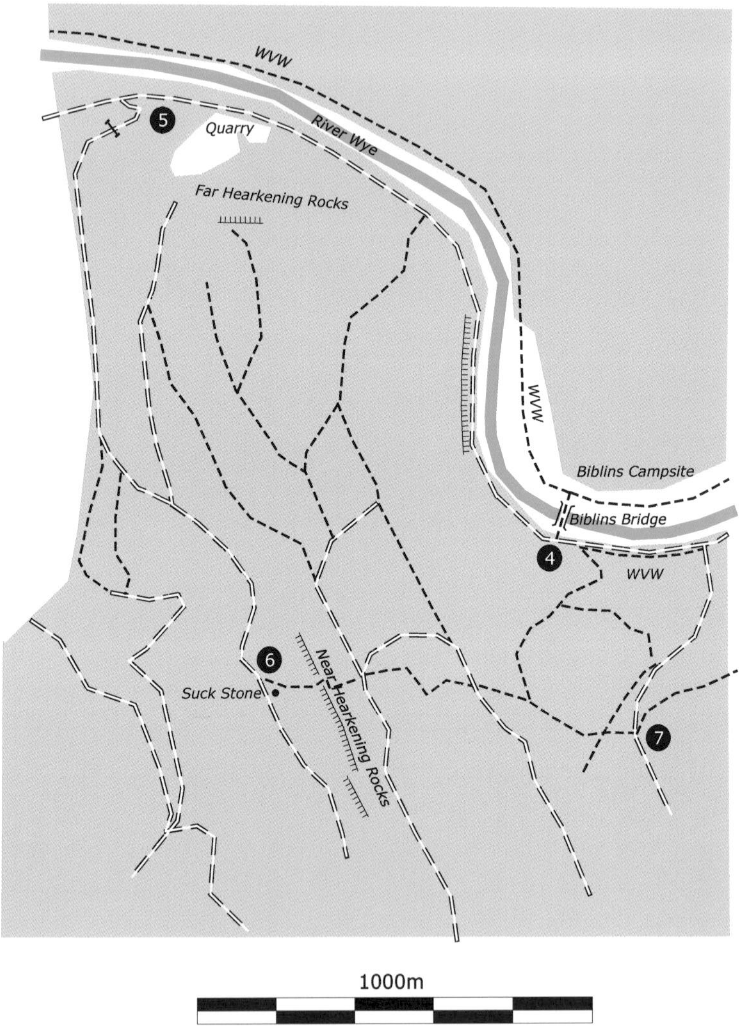

Symonds Yat Map 2

Little Doward from Ganarew

Distance : 4.3km
Difficulty : Moderate

Walk Description Little Doward hill fort sits atop a prominent hill overlooking the Wye. This walk hjas a geology theme as the climbs to the fort passes through exposed outcrops of all the rock layers of the Wye valley. This is one of very few places in the Wye Valley where this is possible. The walk leads up to the hill fort. A map of the hillfort can be seen on page 24 in case you want to explore it. There are some interesting diversions from this walk, for example down to a well-preserved 18c Limekiln and the river Wye. Look out for the many gnarled and curiously-shaped trees in the woods.

How to get there The start of the walk is located just north of Monmouth. Starting at the Dixton roundabout, head north on the A40 towards Ross on Wye. The dual carriageway climbs for two miles, offering occasional glimpses of the wooded slopes of Little Doward on the right. A prominent brick bridge crosses the A40 at the top of the hill. Turn left immediately after the bridge, and follow the road over the bridge to the T junction. Turn left, and the car park is about 100m up the road on the right.

Directions Before leaving the car park have a look at the information board beside the gate as it gives a bit of background to the history of the site.

To start the walk follow the wide and obvious track for 400m to the hairpin bend. The track steepens around the bend but levels out afterwards.

After the hairpin bend ignore the small path that leads off to the left and keep to the track. This takes you to point ❶ at which the track bears left and starts to climb. Leave the track and go straight ahead onto a small path. Follow this path, which offers glimpses of the car park below.

The Tintern Sandstone outcrop at point ❸

After about 250m the path reaches a gate. Many of the gates on this hillside were installed when the hill was part of a long-gone deer park. The wall either side of the gate is much older and dates back to Victorian times when the area was a picturesque park. Significant sections of the Victorian wall still exist and can be spotted throughout the walk.

After the gate the path becomes a pleasant grassy terrace. Ignore the path which climb up the hill to the left and carry on along the path.

After a short distance it starts to descend as it curves slowly around the base of the hill. Part of the Victorian carriage drive and a deer fence come up from Wyastone Leys on the right.

About 150m after the carriage drive the path reaches point ❷, an

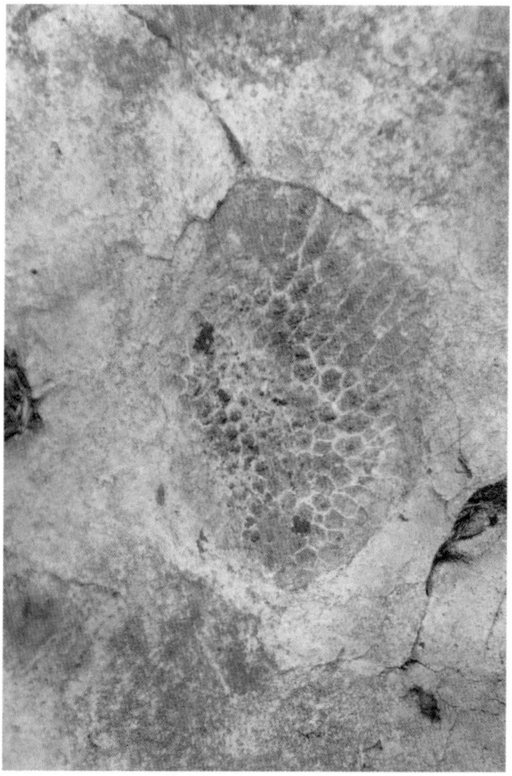

One of several fossils in the Limestone Pavement

outcrop of Quartz Conglomerate. This rock was laid down by running water. Layers containing big pebbles were laid by fast running water, while pebble free layers were deposited in calm water.

Continue along the path for another 50m. About half way between point ❷ and the gate there is an inlet on the left. Its rather overgrown, but on the left wall you can see Quartz Conglomerate and on the right is Tintern Sandstone. This is the boundary between the two rock layers with the more recent sandstone on top.

Go through gate and take the left fork. The path starts to climb and, about 150m after the gate you come to point ❸, the Tintern Sandstone outcrop. A pair of trees have grown through the

exposed rocks.
From point ❸, continue along the path which does a sharp left to a bench, which is most welcome on a humid summer day. Continuing along the path brings you to point ❹, the Dolomitic Limestone outcrop. Generally called 'Dolostone', this limestone includes magnesium as well as calcium and is less reactive than normal limestone when tested with acid.
After another 200m up the track leads to the final outcrop at point ❺. There is a bit of a drop on the right and a dog-sized cave in the outcrop so inquisitive dogs should be put on a lead.
The Oolitic limestone includes patches of crystals which can be seen by closer inspection. There are also some shot-holes where the Victorian workmen blasted through the rock to make the cutting for the path.
Follow rocks through the cutting and keep the rocks on your left. Immediately at the end of the rocks a short steep path goes up left to the limestone pavement ❻. In 2020 there were plans to install steps here so these might be installed by the time of publication. There are several fossils on this limestone pavement, one of which can be seen in the picture on page 21.
After looking at the limestone pavement, return to the path and follow it to a five-way path junction point ❼. Cross the junction and take the wide path up the hill. You'll see a bench at the top of the hill just to the left of the gap in the earthworks at point ❽.
This is not the fort entrance but was made in Victorian times for the scenic carriageway. Take a few moments to rest on the bench and take in the view over the Valley to the woods beyond. On the left, 150m away atop the earthworks, is the trig point marking the highest point of the hill.
Return to the track at point ❽ and carry on down the track to point ❾, pausing to look at the double earthwork and deep ditch.
Follow the track back to point ❶ and the car park.

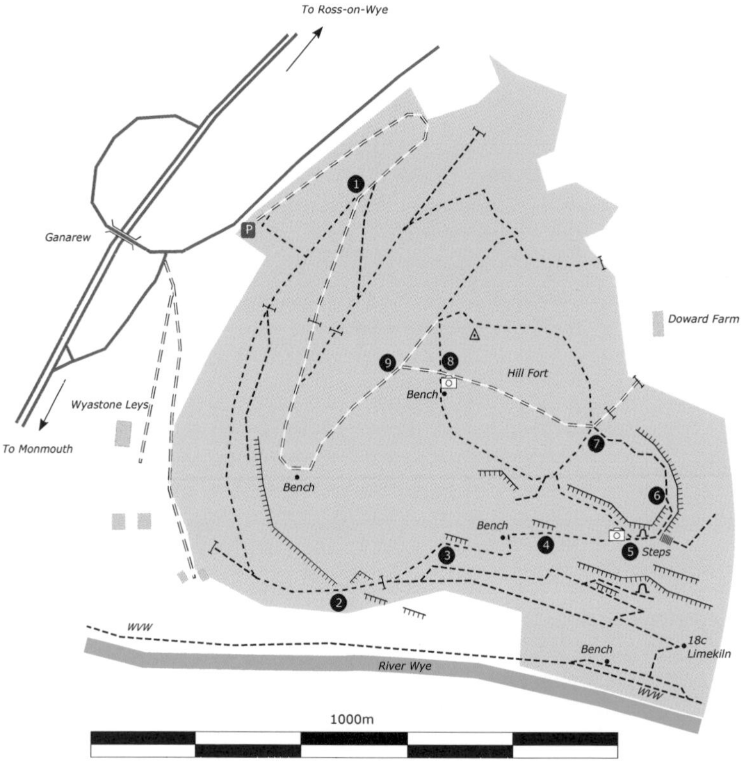

Little Doward from Ganarew Map

Little Doward Hill Fort

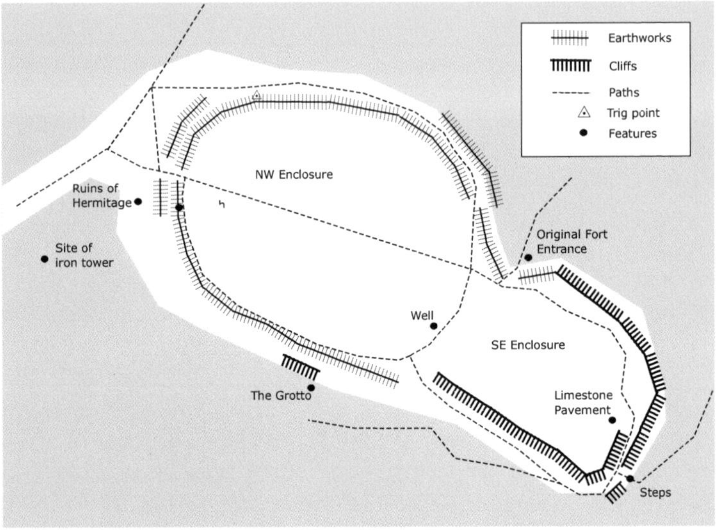

Little Doward Hill Fort is believed to pre-Roman, and was re-occupied after the Roman departure. Geoffrey of Monmouth recounts that the Vortigern, claimant to the title 'King of the Britons', was burned to death in the fort during the fifth century. In Victorian times Richard Blakemore MP owned the site, driving a carriageway up the hillside and building the iron tower, several grottoes and the 'Hermitage'. He is reported to have hired local men to play the hermit, babbling incoherently to visitors. The creation of his park damaged much of the archaeology. The site was designated as a schedule ancient monument in 1928 and has been subject to several archaeological surveys since then.

The site contains two enclosures. The SE enclosure is surrounded by cliffs, and archaeological surveys have found level platforms for houses. The larger NW enclosure has little evidence of building and is believed to be an agricultural enclosure.

Little Doward via King Arthurs Cave

Distance : 3.4km
Difficulty : Hard

Walk Description Little Doward Hill Fort is a wonderful place for walking dogs. This walk ascends the quiet side of the hill, visiting King Arthur's Cave and circling the ramparts of the fort. The paths are steep in places, but they dry quickly after rain. It's a nice place to go for a bit of solitude.

How to get there The start of the walk is located just north of Monmouth. Starting at the Dixton roundabout, head north on the A40 towards Ross on Wye. The dual carriageway climbs for two miles, offering occasional glimpses of the wooded slopes of Little Doward on the right. A prominent brick bridge crosses the A40 at the top of the hill. Turn left immediately after the bridge, and follow the road over the bridge to the T junction. Turn left, and follow the road for about 0.4 miles. After passing some houses on the turn right into a well-concealed single-track road, signposted for Biblins and Doward Park Campsite. Follow this road to the entrance of Doward Park Campsite, about 1 miles from the junction. Turn onto the track and follow into the woods for about 150 yards. There is parking for about 12 cars just beside the sign board.

Directions The first few hundred meters of this walk require a bit of attention. The path meanders a bit, and if you go too far to the left you'll end up going downhill into the valley and have to climb back up. Too far to the right takes you to the top of the caves and a quarry with some nasty drops.
At the end of the car park is a barrier across the track to Biblins Campsite. To the right of the barrier there is a path that enters the woods. To the right of this is a fence which marks the top of the quarry.
Take the path and follow it through the woods, keeping within sight of the edge of the trees on your right. At point ❶ there is a

King Arthur's Cave

fork in the path which sometimes gets covered in leaves. If you see it take the right fork, otherwise just stick to the path. The path drops into an open area with the fence about 30m to your right. As you descend into this area you'll see the caves on your right. You've safely arrived and at point ❷.

From bones and other materials found in the caves, archaeologists believe that the caves were inhabited about 20,000 years ago.

After inspecting the caves go to the fence and turn left, following the path that heads downhill along the fence. At the bottom of the slope you can ignore the small path joins from the right. In spring the woods around this path junction are full of wild garlic.

Continuing along the path you pass a sign for 'Woodland Trust' as you start to go uphill. The path steepens slightly and turns left, then after 50m it steepens again and turns sharp right. Mercifully, it levels out after this bend so you can get your breath back. It does another left turn them after 50m, a path joins from the right. You're now at point ❸.

Turn right onto this path. The cliffs which surround the SE enclosure of the fort are clearly visible through the trees on your left. After 250m the path takes a sharp left hand bend and goes steeply uphill to a gap in the wall, point ❹. Go through the gap and, after about 50m, you arrive at a track. Turn left onto the track and follow it uphill through a farm gate until it levels. This was the original fort entrance point ❺.

On your right the huge NW enclosure stretches uphill. In front and to the left is the SE enclosure, surrounded by cliffs.

Point ❺ is a five-way path junction. Turn sharp right onto a grassy path that leads back towards the woods. The path curves around the outside the the NW enclosure underneath the ramparts. After 250m the path passes beneath the trig point which marks the top of the hill. Shortly after this you reach another path junction, point ❻.

The Steps

Turn left and follow the small path (or the track if the path is a bit overgrown) to the gap in the ramparts. This is not an original entrance to the fort but a gap carved by the Victorians. Just to the right of the gap is a small bench, which is a welcome sight after the long climb.

From the bench carry on a long the top of the ramparts. After 200m the path dips into some scrubby undergrowth at point ❼. Look for small paths that disappear into the bracken on your right. Take the second one, and it leads you right underneath the cliffs to point ❽. If you can't find these two paths, and they can get a bit overgrown in mid summer, just carry on back to point ❺ and turn right down the grassy path to point ❽.

From point ❽ go through a small gap in the fence and descend the steps. If your dog is unhappy with the steps there's a dip in the wall to the right of the steps where you can pick it up and lower it to the ground.

From the steps there is a clear path to point ❸, from which you can retrace your steps to the caves.

From the caves there are two ways back to the car park. One way is just to follow the path to the right of the caves and retrace your steps. The alternative is to to turn left along the track which runs

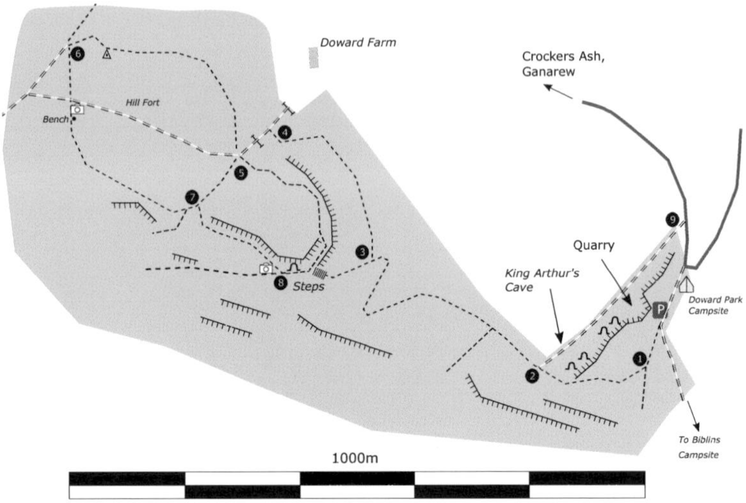

Little Doward From King Arthur's Cave Map

between the fence and the cliffs. This takes you past several other caves and through an old quarry. At the end of the track turn right onto the lane, then right onto the access track to Biblins. The car park is 100m down the track.

Trellech Common

Distance : 4.5km
Difficulty : Easy

Walk Description Trellech Common is an area of woods to the north of Trellech. It has three car parks around the edge so it offers many opportunities for walks, of which this is one. Its popular with local dog walkers so expect to meet a few people and dogs along the way. This walk is a winter favourite as the forestry tracks dry quickly after rain.

How to get there Leave Trellech on the B4293 towards Monmouth. After about 1¼ miles turn right onto a road signposted 'The Narth, Pennarth, Whitebrook'. The car park is about 200m down this road on the right.

Directions Two picnic tables were installed in the car park in 2019. A small but obvious path winds uphill from the middle of the car park, passing one of the picnic tables. Follow this path through the trees for about 150m until it meets a track at point ❶.
Turn left onto this track and follow it for about 700m, passing a disused quarry on the right. About 500m from point ❶ the path dips slightly, and there is a spring in the trees on the left. I try to keep Holly out of the spring as it's full of rotting vegetation all year round and she usually smells rather ripe afterwards.
A path crosses the track at point ❷. Turn left onto the path which climbs gently through an avenue of trees. After 200m the path narrows, and bears slightly left to a small car park at point ❸.
Turn left onto a broad track and follow it for 1km to a T-junction with another track at point ❹. The walk turns left here and follows the track to the start, passing a small pool on the bend at point ❺.
For a longer walk turn right at point ❹. This takes you to another car park and onto a quiet lane through Maryland onto Beacon Hill where it can be linked to the walk around Beacon Hill in chapter 5.

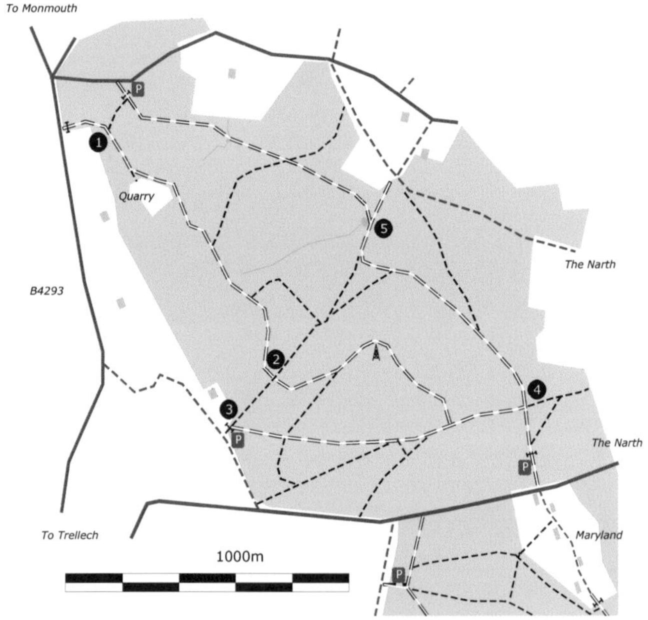

Trellech Common Map

Beacon Hill

Distance : 4.8km
Difficulty : Easy

Walk Description This pleasant walk explores an area of woodland and reclaimed heathland, linking several good viewpoints. Its accessibility and good paths have made Beacon Hill a popular area with local dog walkers and horse riders. Holly particularly likes the pond towards the end of the walk, the site of many games of swimmy fetch. There are a few, avoidable, muddy sections on the paths in the winter.

Note that this walk is located between Trellech Common, chapter 4, and Bargain Wood, chapter 7. The maps for the three chapters have been drawn to show the links between these walks.

How to get there Leave Trellech on the road signposted to Llandogo and Catbrook, and immediately fork left off the Catbrook road. Follow this for about half a mile then turn left onto the narrow lane. Follow this lane uphill for a quarter of a mile and you'll find Beacon View car park on the right.

Directions Take a few minutes to enjoy the view from the car park. Trellech can be seen clearly in front of you, with the spire of St Nicholas Church dominating the town. To the right you can see the the distinctive shapes of Sugar Loaf and Black Mountains about 20 miles away.

Go through the fence to the notice board and follow the path as it leads gently uphill into the woods, passing a picnic table on your left.

Continue to follow the path until you come to the gate at point ❶. Go through the gate onto the heathland, and follow the path as it crosses a wide track. The path gently descends towards a line of pine trees. After passing through a second gate you come to a T-junction with a waypost. Turn right onto the path and follow it along the edge of the heath to the path junctions at point ❷.

Members of the Editorial Board on the Boulders at point ❸

Note that turning left onto the track takes you through Maryland and connects to the Trellech Common walk in chapter 4.
Turn left at point ❷ and, after about 30m, cross the track onto another wide track. Follow this track for about 250m to a barrier. After the barrier there is a line of boulders on the right, point ❸. Take the path which goes into the woods beside the last boulder.
Follow this path through the woods to point ❹. The end of tyhe path can get a bit muddy in winter, but walkers usually make a path around the mud to the right.
At point ❹ turn right onto the track which follows Offa's Dyke Path and, after 100m, there will be a small gap in the trees. Go through this gap to a bench, and enjoy the amazing view. Directly opposite you is St Briavels Common, and to the right you can see nine miles down the valley to the old Severn Bridge. Pictures of this view are often found in articles and guides for Offa's Dyke path.
Rejoining the track, continue for 500m to the next track junction at point ❺ where there is another bench, and abundant blackberry bushes in summer.
Note that the left hand fork at point ❺ leads to Cleddon Falls. This can be a nice diversion after rain when the falls are in full flow. This path also connects with the Bargain Wood walk in chapter 7.
Continuing along the main track leads to a steel barrier and a T-junction. Turn right at the barrier and follow the track up the hill to the fork in the tracks at point ❻.
Take the left fork and you'll see a cattle grid in front of you. This can be bypassed through the gate on its right. Just past the cattle grid there is a prominent dead tree trunk on the heath on the right.

The view down the valley to the Old Severn Bridge nine miles away

This tree marks the pond, which is one of Holly's favourite places. In spring you need to watch your step as there can be hundreds of new frogs taking their first steps around the edge of the pond.
Continue along this track to a bench on the left. Take a moment to enjoy the view across to the Malverns and the Cotswolds before turning left. Go down the track to the gates at point ❼.
There are several paths after the gate, but one goes off about 45 degrees to the right. Take this path to the summit of Beacon Hill, which is marked by a trig point in the woods. This is the highest point in Monmouthshire. Travelling east at at this latitude the next point at this altitude is in the Ural Mountains in Russia.
Shortly after the trig point there is a T-junction where you turn left to get back to the car park.

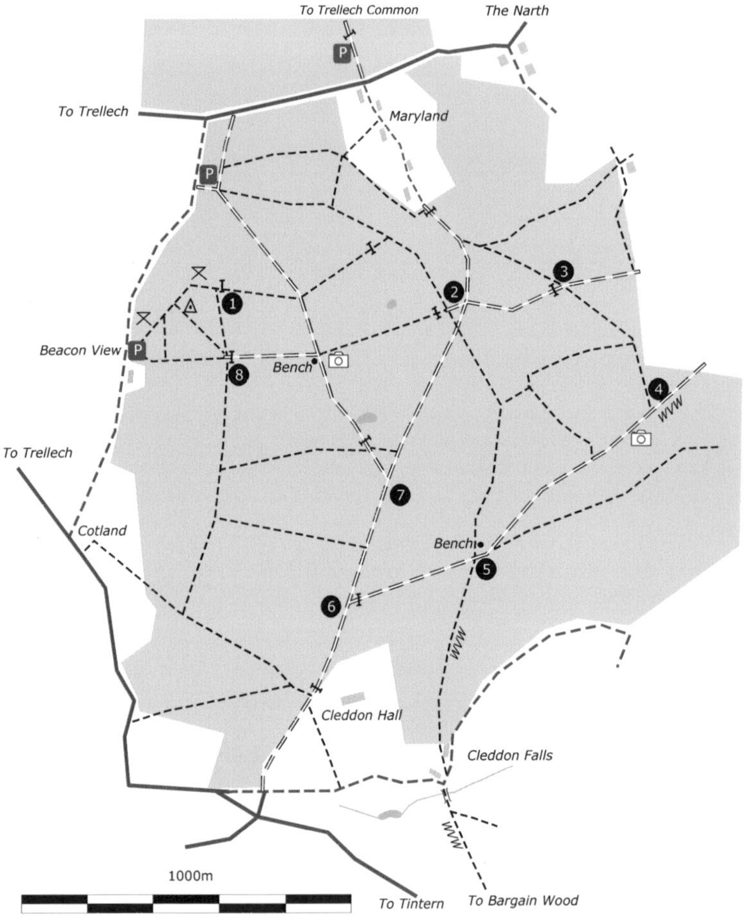

Beacon Hill Map

Ninewells Wood

Distance : 3.1km
Difficulty : Easy

Walk Description This walk is a pleasant and gentle stroll in woodland, far away from the traffic noise. The mix of natural woods and pinewoods, and its proximity to Cleddon Bog nature reserve, means that it supports a good variety of birds.

In winter its advisable to wear boots for the occasional muddy sections, especially between points ❸ and ❹. The stiles can be easily bypassed by dogs.

How to get there Leave Trellech on the road signposted to Llandogo and Catbrook, and immediately fork left off the Catbrook road. Follow this road for about 1¼ miles. Ignore the narrow road to Cleddon which forks to the left, and Ninewells Wood car park is about 200m on the right.

Directions Leave the car park and bypass the forestry barrier through the kissing gate. This takes you onto a nice gravel track which runs through the middle of the woods.

After the gate the path starts a gentle curve to the right. When it straightens there is a small path going into the woods on the left. This is point ❶. Ignore that path for now - you'll be coming back up it later.

The track now heads more or less straight through the middle of the woods so navigation for the next 1km is really easy. The woods are mainly broad leaf, interspersed with plantations of conifers. The trees have been cleared for the first 200m, and if you look over you right shoulder you get glimpses of Cleddon Hall - birthplace of the philosopher Bertrand Russell.

After 1km there is the first of four stiles, all easily bypassed. In 2020 the fence had been removed on the right of this stile. Even if the fence is restored there is still plenty of room for a dog to pass

The steps in the woods; are they man-made?

under it.
The gravel track ends at this first stile and it becomes a normal path through the woods. At the second stile a house can be seen through trees on the right. I usually put Holly on a lead when I first see the house as the path is getting close to the Trellech-Catbrook lane.
At the end of the woods are the remains of a stone wall, so low that a Labrador could step over it. This is point ❷.
Turn sharp left before the lane onto another path through the woods. After about 150m you'll see the first of two stiles. Path goes between two fences to the last stile by two bungalows, point ❸. Dogs can easily get under both of these stiles.
Cross the access road to the bungalows and go through the gate opposite into the woods. This next section of the path can be narrow and gets muddy after rain, but only the for the first 150m. The woods to the right of this path were bought privately in 2013 and are being restored to natural woodland.
After 150m the view starts to open up on the right to show some large fields bordered by impressively large trees. The path leads to a gate at point ❹, through which the path continues to Catbrook. Turn left at the gate and follow the fence for 200m to another gate

at point ❺.
Turn left again and follow the fence slightly downhill to the path crossing at point ❻. The path to the left goes back to the bungalows while straight ahead goes to the gravel track through the woods.
Turn right and follow the fence along the edge of the woods. Eventually the fence is replaced by a stone wall at point ❼.
There are many ways back to the gravel track, which is slightly downhill to the left. The sign points down to the left, but there's a quieter path straight ahead. Carry on straight and keep the wall about 5m on your right.
After about 100m the path bends left and the wall bends to the right. Continue on this small path to another path junction. The sign has loads of arrows but ignore them all and go straight ahead.
Continue along the small path. About half way along the path there is a set of stone steps. These look man-made, rather like a garden feature, but why would anyone make some steps in the middle of the woods?
At the next path junction, point ❽ turn left and take the path back to point ❶. Turn right and the track takes you back to the car park.

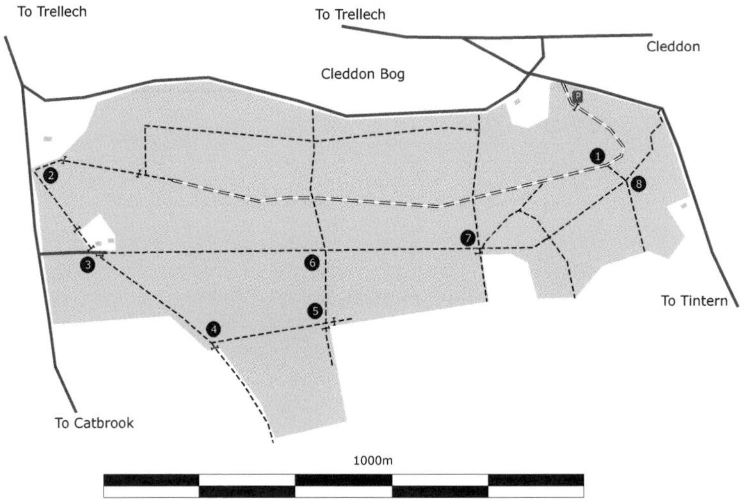

Ninewells Wood Map

The River Wye

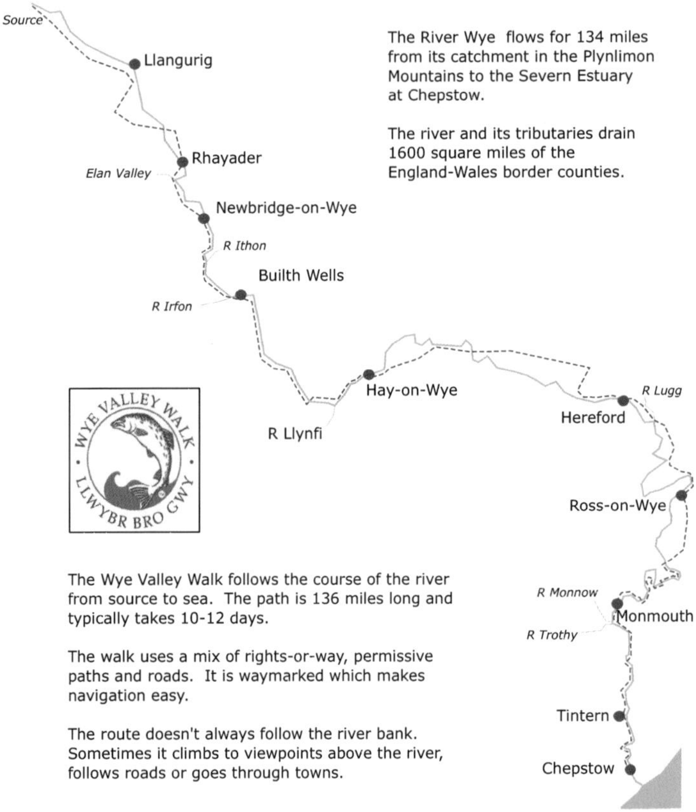

The River Wye flows for 134 miles from its catchment in the Plynlimon Mountains to the Severn Estuary at Chepstow.

The river and its tributaries drain 1600 square miles of the England-Wales border counties.

The Wye Valley Walk follows the course of the river from source to sea. The path is 136 miles long and typically takes 10-12 days.

The walk uses a mix of rights-or-way, permissive paths and roads. It is waymarked which makes navigation easy.

The route doesn't always follow the river bank. Sometimes it climbs to viewpoints above the river, follows roads or goes through towns.

Bargain Wood

Distance : 1.6km
Difficulty : Easy

With extension to Cleddon Distance : 2.5km
Difficulty : Easy

Walk Description

This short walk is very popular with dog walkers. It starts at the Whitestone car park, which includes a picnic area and children's play area. The walk follows good tracks and includes several fine viewpoints. The optional extension to Cleddon Falls is worthwhile, particularly after rain when they can be quite spectacular.

How to get there

From Trellech: Leave on the road signposted to Llandogo and Catbrook, and immediately fork left off the Catbrook road. Follow this road for 2.2 miles, following signs for Llandogo. Whitestone car park is on the left.

From Tintern: Turn off the A466 on by the Wye Valley Pub, signposted towards Catbrook. Follow this lane for 1.5 miles to a T-junction. Whitestone car park is directly in front of you.

Directions

Route finding on this walk is really easy. From the car park ❶ head uphill along the track, passing the picnic site on your right. This takes you to the steel barrier ❷. After the barrier the track continues to climb and curve to the left. At the top of the slope it straightens into a long, broad, track.

As you go along the track there are three viewpoints on your right, each with a bench. These all face north-west towards the Hudnalls, overlooking the river. The last viewpoint looks along the river and partly up the valley to Mork. After the last viewpoint the track turns sharply to the left, almost doubling back on itself ❸.

There is an optional excursion here to Cleddon Falls. The stream

Autumn View from Bargain Wood

runs all the way down the hillside to the Wye in a series of small waterfalls. They are well worth a visit a day or two after rain. Turn right for the falls, then retrace your steps to point ❸ to continue the walk. Note that the walk to Cleddon Falls can be further extended by adding a walk around Beacon Hill, chapter 5.

To return to the car park leave point ❸ on the broad track through the woods. After a 600m the track turns sharply to the right. Ignore this turn and continue straight ahead down a rocky path to the car park.

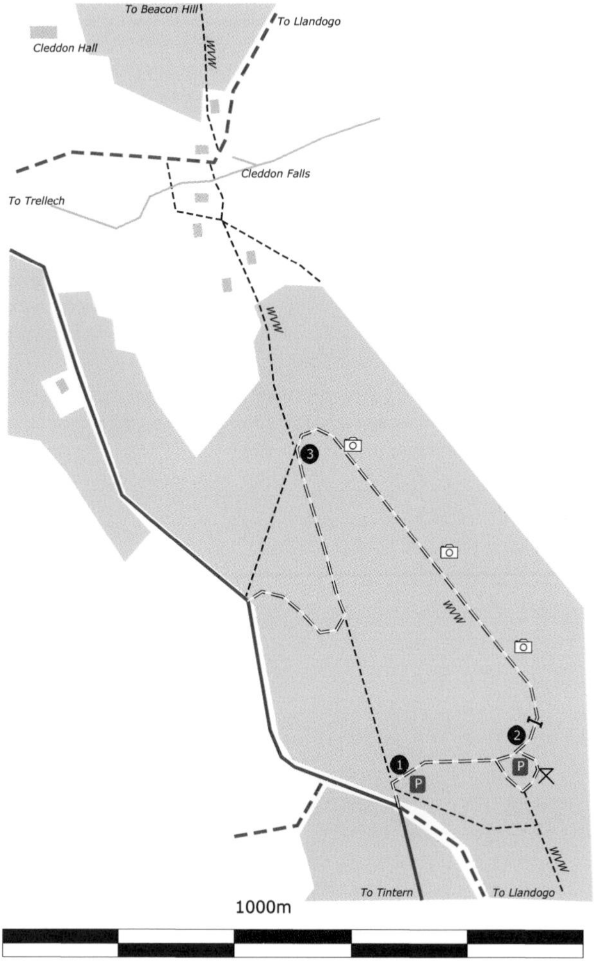

Bargain Wood Map

The Industrial River

The River Wye was a major trading route for coal and iron from the Forest of Dean, as well as wood and limestone. The Romans were the first to exploit these resources. Organised exploitation started in Elizabethan times.

By the early 1800s the lower Wye and its side valleys had become highly industrialised. Whitebrook became the base of a thriving paper industry. Redbrook was named because its waters ran red with the outpourings of its iron works. The Angiddy valley above Tintern was the home to a successful wireworks, the preserved ruins of which are accessible to walkers. Lime quarries and kilns were found all along the river, and their remains are often encountered in riverside walks. Many of these industries continued through to the early 20th century.

Restored Limekiln at Little Doward *(See map on page 23)*

Goods were initially transported along the river in flat bottomed boats. They were transshipped to coastal boats at Brockweir to cross the estuary to Bristol. This continued until 1824 when a road was built from St Arvans to Redbrook. Capacity was further increased when the Wye Valley Railway started operations in 1876. The line carried passengers until 1959 and continued operations to serve the lime quarries until 1990. The tracks have been removed, but many sections of the line remain in use as cycleways and paths.

Offa's Dyke and The Sunken Road

Distance : 6.8km
Difficulty : Hard

Walk Description This is a lovely, quiet, walk with a historical theme. The walk starts a few miles north of the tourist spots of Tintern. The route takes advantage of Offa's Dyke Path on the outward leg, and follows an ancient sunken road on the return leg. Just above Coxbury farm there is a lovely view back up the valley to Bigsweir Bridge.
The path is a bit rough underfoot at times and can get muddy after rain, especially along the sunken road.

How to get there The walk starts a few miles north of Tintern. At the eastern end of Bigsweir Bridge take the small road that forks off the A466 sign-posted to Mork and St Briavels. Follow this road for about a quarter of a mile and there is a small car park for Cadora Woods on the left. Note that the car park has a 2m headroom.

Directions At the at the rear of the car park, ignore the main track through the gate, and instead take the small path through the woods at the rear right hand side. The path is marked with the acorn sign for Offa's Dyke Path. Take this path and follow it through the trees for about 100m where it meets the end of a small lane. The route continues through the gap beside the gate, following the signs for Offa's Dyke, to the path junction at point ❶. Take the left hand fork, as shown by the Offa's Dyke Path marker on the wooden post. Note that the right fork is the path that you will return on.
Continue along the path as it gently climbs through mixed woodland. After a while the path descends slightly to a gate at point ❷.
Leave the woods through the gate and continue to follow Offa's Dyke Path as it follows the edge of the fields through a series of kissing gates. This section can get a bit muddy after rain, but

Looking along the sunken road

muddy sections can usually be bypassed by going slightly uphill. The path goes gradually uphill through a short section of woods the path emerges with the buildings of Coxbury Farm visible in front to the right. There are several gaps in the trees from this point onwards, offering pleasant views across the Wye to Lower Hael Wood.

Continue across the fields until the path meets a fence and turns sharply right through a kissing gate into a copse. There are some remnants of the earthworks of Offas Dyke in this copse. The path follows the bottom of the ditch and you can see the remains of the earth rampart alongside the path.

Passing through a wooden gate you arrive at point ❸. Offa's Dyke Path continues straight ahead into Highbury Wood Nature Reserve, but our walk turns right onto Coxbury and Wyegate Lane. This sunken road was the main route from Monmouth to St Briavels in medieval times, following the eastern ridge above the Wye Valley.

Continuing along the sunken road leads to an unusual feature at point ❹, a sunken road junction. Meanwhile views are starting to open up on both sides of the track. To the right is the Wye Valley, and the left is a charming valley that runs from Newlands, carrying a small stream that joins the Wye at Redbrook.

The sunken road ends near the entrance to Coxbury Farm, after which the road becomes partly metalled. It's time to get the camera out as, about 100m after the farm entrance a panoramic

The view down to Bigsweir Bridge

view of the valley opens up across the fields. At the bottom of the valley, dwarfed by the wooded valley sides, is Bigsweir bridge.
The track eventually becomes fully metalled providing an access lane to the farm and its fields. Continue along the track for 800m with woodland on your right. The track does a sharp left and right turn then leads you into Wyegate Green, point ❺. Pass straight through this hamlet and take the track directly in front of you. About 200m after leaving Wyegate Green the track turns left to some fields. Leave the track and go straight ahead onto the small path .

The path descends on (occasionally) uneven ground between two fields. Some attempts have been made to lay rocks on this path to prvoide a drier and more even surface. As it starts to descend to the Mork valley you will see a belt of trees about 200m ahead on the right. Continue to descend the track until, in these trees, you see a metal handrail where another path breaks right, point ❻. Take this path to the right and follow it along the field edge, enjoying the views to the left over the Mork Valley.

The path widens on entering the woods and slowly descends back to point ❶, from which it is a short walk back to the car park.

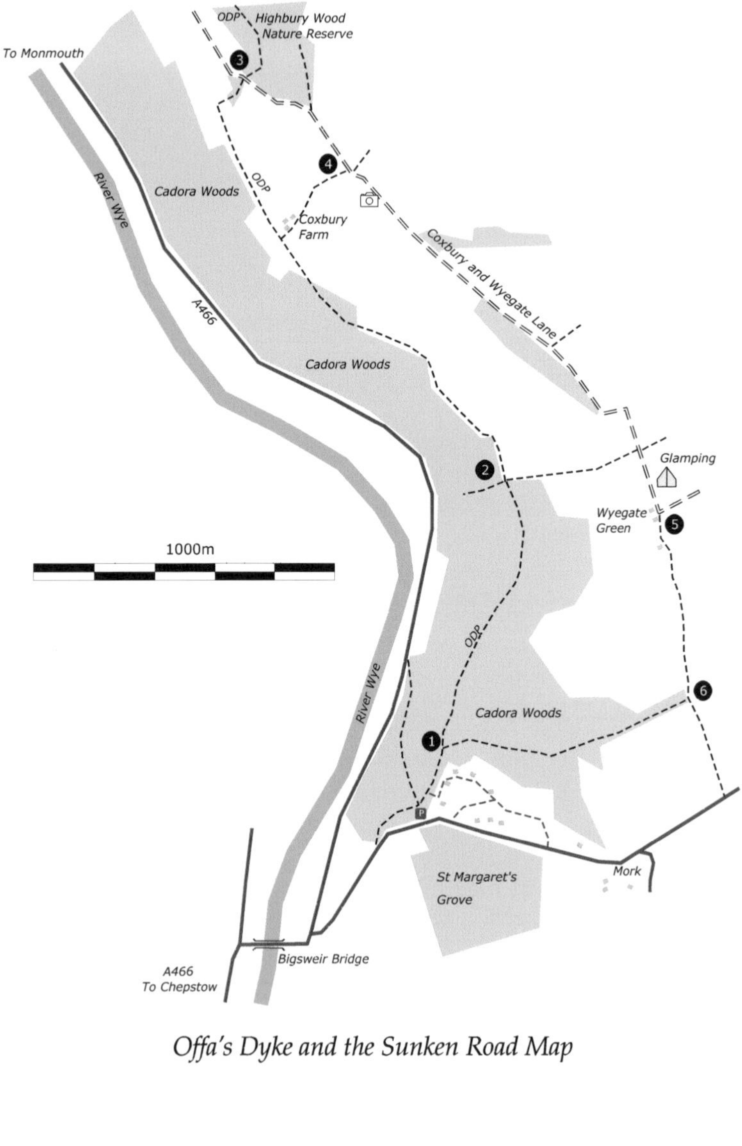

Offa's Dyke and the Sunken Road Map

Brockweir and the Old Station

Distance : 5.6km
Difficulty : Moderate

Walk Description

This walk starts at the Old Station, Tintern. Once a main station on the Chepstow to Monmouth line it is now a popular tourist attraction with a dog-friendly cafe and ample parking.

The walk takes you across the Grade II listed Brockweir bridge into Brockweir village. After leaving the village the walk zig-zags through the woods, taking the easiest paths up to Offa's Dyke Path. Emerging from the woods there is a impressive view over Brockweir and across the valley to St Briavels Common. The walk follows Offa's Dyke Path across the fields to the village and back to the start.

There are four stiles along the route but they can all be bypassed by dogs. Refreshments and poop bins can be found at the Old Station.

How to get there

The Old Station is about half a mile north of Tintern on the A466. In 2016 the charge was £1.00 for three hours parking and £3.50 all day.

Directions

Start at the cafe and head along the platform towards the water tower and signal gantry. At the signal gantry, point ❶, there is a flight of steps leading down to the fields alongside the river.

If the river is low, and there are no sheep in the field, then you can go through the riverside fields to Brockweir Bridge. Otherwise you can continue along the track past some interesting artwork to the end of the bridge.

This can be a lovely spot on an early morning. The old bridge, the whitewashed cottages, and the cirque of wooded hills give this place a feeling of stillness and history.

Depending on the state of the tide you might see the river flowing upstream at this point.

Remains of the nineteenth century quay at Brockweir

Head up the steps and cross the bridge into Brockweir village. Now tranquil, the village was once a busy port where goods were transshipped between river boats and coastal craft. It was a lawless town with over a dozen pubs, so the Duke of Beaufort established a Moravian Church in an attempt to civilise the village. As you cross the bridge you can see the remains of the quay on the left, and the Moravian Church on the right.

On entering the village you'll pass the Brockweir Country Inn ❷ on your right. In 2019 the inn was closed for structural repairs but the owners plan to re-open. The Inn is dog friendly and has a courtyard out the back. Turn immediately right onto the small lane beside the inn.

After 50m there is bridge over the mill race. If the river is high go along the lane onto the "Restricted Byway". If the river is low then you can take a more pleasant route along the bank by taking the small path on the right just before the bridge. This takes you past some cottages and the Moravian Church, leading over a stile into the field. The stile can be bypassed by dogs. Follow the path along the riverbank until it turns sharp left to a stile in the hedge, at which point it rejoins the Restricted Byway.

The byway slowly climbs from the river. In spring the slopes on both sides of the path are covered in wild garlic and bluebells.

About 600m after the stile you'll come to a low wall on your right. This is point ❸. At this point you want to turn sharply left and continue to gently climb up the valley side. After 50m there is a fork in the path and a signpost. Take the left fork, following signs

The view over Brockweir. The bridge is in the bottom left of the picture

for "Beeches Campsite".

This path gently climbs through the woods until, after abut 900m, another path crosses it. Turn left onto this path and follow it until you reach the junction with Offa's Dyke Path, point ❹. In front of you is the gate leading to Beeches Farm and the campsite. Turn left onto Offa's Dyke path towards Brockweir and the Hudnalls.

The path follows the edge of the woods, with the fields of Beeches Farm on the right. Follow Offa's Dyke Path to a stile, that is easily bypassed by dogs. About 100m after the stile there is a wooden ramp and steps that take Offa's Dyke Path down into the fields, point ❹. At the end of the ramp there is a big step down into the field so small dogs should take care.

The sudden view is delightful. Way down to the left you can see Brockweir village, the bridge and the river. In front of you is St Briavels Common, a hillside covered with small lanes and houses.

Take the obvious path through the grass to the bottom right hand corner of the field. This takes you to the final stile, point ❺. Dogs can bypass this by going through the roots of the small tree on the right of the stile

Continue to follow this track downhill. After 100m it curves to the left, and an Offa's Dyke Path sign shows the way back to Brockweir.

On entering Brockweir at point ❻ turn you turn left into the village and Brockweir Country Inn. Retrace your steps across the bridge, then descend the steps to return to the Old Station.

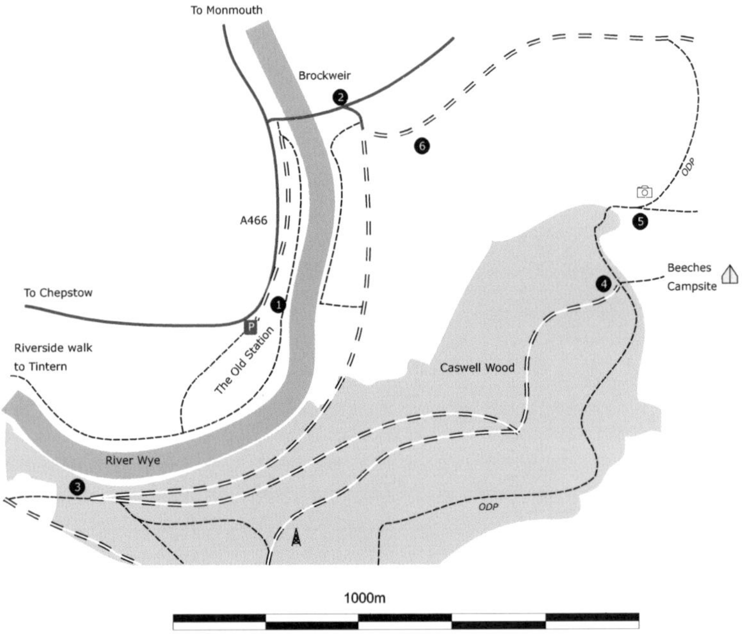

Brockweir and the Old Station Map

Devil's Pulpit from Tintern

Distance : 8.8km
Difficulty : Hard

Walk Description

This walk starts in Tintern and takes you to one of the great viewpoints over the Wye Valley, the Devil's Pulpit. Legend has it that the devil would stand on this prominent rock and try to tempt the monks of Tintern Abbey. Most walking guides take a direct route from Tintern to the Devil's Pulpit, but there are alternatives that use less frequented tracks and paths. This walk is graded hard as it has a lot of ascent, and significant stretches of rough paths.

The walk can be linked with the "Brockweir and the Old Station" walk (chapter 9) for a spectacular long walk.

Dogs and muddy walkers are welcome at the Rose and Crown Pub, just north of Abbey Mills on the A466. There is a poop bin on the main road by Abbey Mills.

How to get there

The walk starts at Abbey Mills in the middle of Tintern. There is free parking in two parking bays on the riverbanks, a few hundred meters north of Abbey Mills. Pay parking is available at Tintern Abbey to the south of Abbey Mills.

Directions

Starting at Abbey Mills, point ❶, walk up the lane and cross the river at the footbridge. This was once a railway bridge that connected the Tintern Wireworks to the Chepstow to Monmouth line. After crossing the bridge the lane bends around to the right and runs parallel with the river.

After about 200m there are a few metal poles on the left where a path breaks off uphill to the left. The path is signposted for Offa's Dyke and Devils Pulpit. Take this path and follow it uphill over rocky ground until it levels off alongside a low wall at point ❷.

Many paths come together at this point and there are three path junctions in a very short distance. Its important to take the correct path.

Tintern Abbey from Devils Pulpit

Start at the low wall, take the right fork that goes slightly uphill, ignore the left fork signposted "Brockweir". Almost immediately there is another junction marked by a metal pole. Take the right fork signposted Offa's Dyke.
The final path junction could go almost unnoticed. Look for a small wooden waypost. The broad path appears to go straight through the woods, however you want turn left onto a small path signposted with the yellow acorn sign for Offa's Dyke.
This path climbs up through the woods and goes up some rocky steps before levelling out and joining a big track at point ❸. Turn right onto the track, ignoring the path that breaks off to the left.
Follow the broad track, known as "Passage Grove", across the hillside through some nice mixed woodland. Along the left hand side of the path there are a few hidden pools where the gundogs like Holly can splash about in muddy water. Looking up through the trees you catch occasional glimpses of Shorn Cliff. After 2km you reach a track junction, point ❹ where you fork left onto the track that heads uphill.
Follow this track uphill for about 1km. Just as it starts to level off there is a wooden signpost on the left. This is point ❺, and

you want to turn left onto Offa's Dyke Path, signposted "Devil's Pulpit 1 Mile".

The path is very easy to follow. There is some steep ground on the left, but the path runs well back from the cliffs. After about 1km the path goes through a gap in a dry stone wall, after which there is a lovely viewpoint on the left. Continuing along the path you quickly reach the Devils Pulpit. Stay a while to admire the view, and try to imagine the devil yelling temptations at the monks!

Walking on, there is a junction where another path heads across the fields to Tidenham Chase. Ignore this, and take a sharp left and follow the path down some steps and across a small bridge, following signs for Tintern and Brockweir.

After about 800m you come to another path junction, point ❻. The path goes straight ahead along Offa's Dyke Path to point ❼. It takes you through some lovely woodland but the last 100m before point ❼ gets slippery when wet.

Carrying on along Offa's Dyke takes you past Lippets Grove Nature Reserve, a site well known for its wild flowers. The path eventually descends to the junction at point ❼, where there are plenty of signs offering you guidance. Offa's Dyke carries on ahead, while the path to the right goes to Beeches Campsite. Our route goes left on a broad path heading downhill.

After a little while we come to the fork at point ❽, where we take the right hand path heading downhill. The bottom of this path takes you back to the low wall at point ❷. Go straight ahead on familiar paths to take you downhill and back to Abbey Mills.

Extension When you get to point ❼ it is possible to extend this walk through Brockweir. Point ❼ is also point ❹ on the "Brockweir and the Old Station" route. Follow the route from that point back to the Old Station, after which there is a riverside path that takes you back to Tintern.

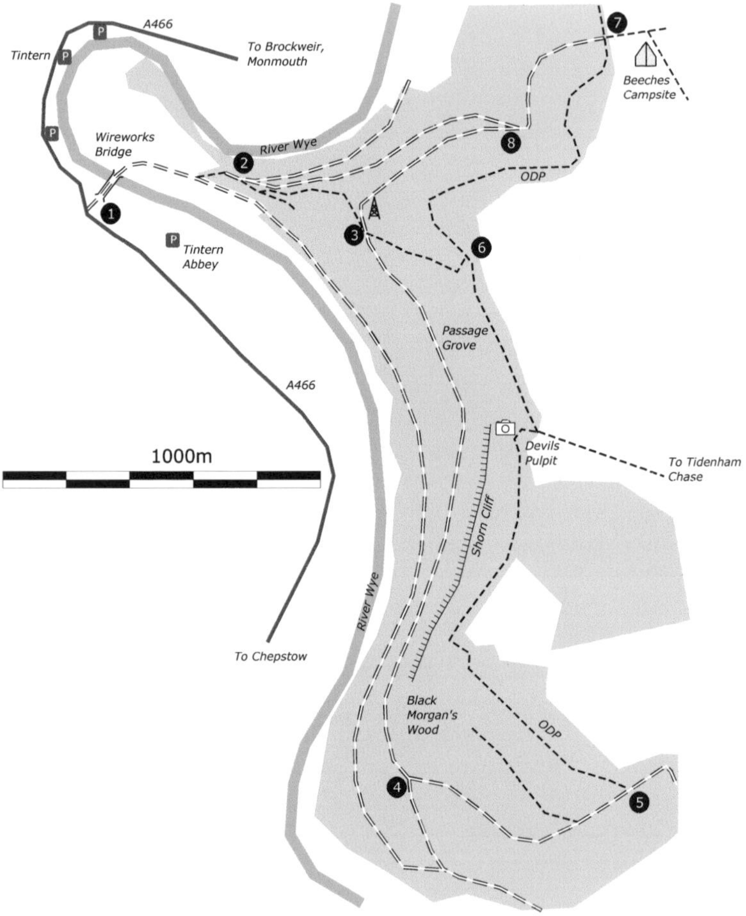

Devil's Pulpit Map

Chepstow Park

Distance (short route): 6.4km
Difficulty : Moderate
Distance (long route): 8.3km
Difficulty : Moderate

Walk Description Chepstow Park is a large area of woodland a few miles north of Chepstow. It has a good network of quick-drying forestry tracks, making this a good venue for walks in the winter.
Two walks are described in this chapter. The first, shorter, walk takes in some of the best features on the woods without losing too much height. The second walk extends the short walk towards Itton, including a lovely viewpoint over Chepstow and the Severn Bridges.

How to get there From Chepstow: Take the A466 north towards Tintern. After passing the racecourse and the Piercefield pub take the left turn into St Arvans. After about two miles a road comes in from the right leading to The Cot. Chepstow Park car park is on the left just after this road.
From Monmouth: Take the B4293 south passing through Trellech, Llanishen and Devauden. At Devauden green ignore the right turn for Itton and Chepstow, continuing on the main road towards St Arvans. Chepstow Park car park is about a mile on the right hand side.
There is space for about 15 cars.

Directions Leave the car park beside the iron gate and head up the gently sloping track. After about 200m you reach point ❶. Ignore the track that joins from the right and continue straight ahead. The track bends to the right and gently climbs to the T-junction at point ❷.
Turn left at point ❷ and go along the edge of the woods, enjoying the occasional views across the fields towards the hill Maen Gaer.

The view from Chepstow Park Woods to the Severn Bridges

After a little while the track takes you to the T-junction at point ❸. This is the decision point between the short and long routes. Turning left takes you right around the edge of the woods to point ❹, whereas turning right takes you on a shorter route past the reservoir.

The Short Route

Turn right at point ❸ and follow the track for 300m. Ignore the track that joins from the right and follow the straight track in front of you.

About 200m after the track junction the track does a small jiggle to the left. You'll see the earth bank of the reservoir in the trees in front of you. Take the small path that climbs the reservoir bank and you'll find a wooden bench on your left. This sheltered pond is lovely on a still day in autumn when the trees are reflected in the water.

On leaving the reservoir, continue along the track to the next track junction. Take the left hand track and continue to follow it until a track that comes in from the left. You are now at point ❺ where the long and short routes meet. Continue straight ahead, ignoring the track that joins you from the left.

Holly enjoying an autumn swim in the reservoir

The Long Route

Turn left at point ❸ and follow the track for about 100m. Just as the track bends to the right, a small path breaks off to a pair of benches. Its a nice spot to rest and enjoy the fabulous view across Chepstow, the Severn bridges and the estuary.

Return to the track and follow as it winds through the trees for about 1.5km. Eventually a track will join you from the right, and you'll see a barrier about 100m in front of you. You've reached point ❹, so turn right onto the track and follow for 1km it as it rises gently to a t-junction. You are now at point ❺ where the long and short routes meet. Turn left at the T-junction.

From point ❺ to the end

Shortly after point ❺ you'll see an opening in the trees on the left. On a clear day there is a view across to Blorenge, Sugar Loaf and the Black Mountains.

After 100m the track will start to go downhill. At the top of the hill a path crosses the track at point ❻. Turn right onto this path, following the blue arrow on the pole and follow it for 200m to the junction at point ❼. You want to turn left at this point, ignoring the long, straight, track in front of you (going straight ahead takes you back to point ❷).

Continue down the track to the next T-junction at point ❽. Turn right here and follow the track.

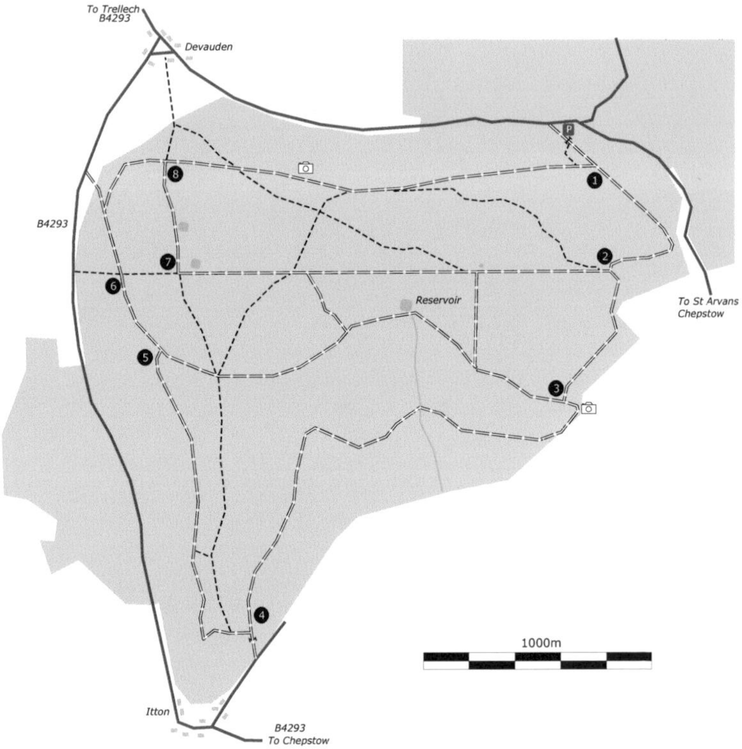

Chepstow Park Map

On the left of the track, about 500m after point ❽, extensive tree felling in 2019 opened up a nice view over Devauden to Beacon Hill. Look carefully on a clear day and you can see the spire of Trellech church.

Continue along the track for another 1.5km to point ❶, from where it is a short walk down the hill to the car park.

Barnets Wood

Distance : 3.2km
Difficulty : Easy

Walk Description Barnets Wood is located just outside Chepstow and is popular with local dog owners. In the spring the light shining through the young beech leaves falls onto a carpet of bluebells and wild garlic. There are many paths to explore, and this easy walk does a gentle excursion around the most accessible parts of the woods.

Not far from Barnets Wood is a small pool in a shallow stream, just behind Coppice Mawr car park. This place is very popular for rinsing off muddy dogs and has been nicknamed "the launderette" by some local dog owners.

How to get there There is a Budgens store at the intersection of the A466 and B4235, about 100m south of Chepstow Racecourse. Turn onto the B4235 at the store and follow it for just over a mile. The entrance to Great Barnets Wood car park is on the left, just before the end of the woods.

Directions From the car park entrance you can see a barrier directly ahead of you, point ❶ on the map. Start at this barrier, but ignore the obvious track in front of you. Instead you should head through the trees on your right, keeping the fence along the edge of the woods in sight.

The path curves around to the left, and continues close to the edge of the woods. As a general rule, if you can see the fence on your right then you're on the right path. Ignore the path that comes in from the left at point ❷ and continue straight ahead. Shortly after point ❷ there is a large depression that can be passed on the right hand side.

After passing the depression the the path continues through the trees for another few hundred meters until it meets a track.

Turn left along the track (there are no other options!) and follow it for 300m until it bends sharply to the left at point ❸. You have

Bluebells in Barnets Wood

two choices for getting to point ❺. The easy option is to continue along the track where, after 30m a path cuts right into the trees to point ❺. If, however, you have good grip on your shoes then take the path that goes straight ahead off the bend. After 100m it drops steeply down into a narrow valley, curving around to the right after the steepest bit.

At the bottom of the steep path you cross a small stream that is almost dry in summer, and can be jumped in winter. You are at point ❹. The sides of this narrow valley are covered with wild garlic in the spring. Turn left up the valley with the stream on your left, taking the left fork after about 300m. The path curves to the left and gently climbs to point ❺. From point ❺ carry on along the track to point ❻.

At the track junction, point ❻, turn left and follow the track back to the car park.

"The Launderette"

If your dog likes splashing around in streams then you might like complete this walk with a visit to "The Launderette". The launderette is a shady section of stream that is shallow with gentle banks. A bridge crosses the stream at this point. Its a perfect spot for playing water games with dogs, cooling them down on a hot day, or just rinsing off the mud.

To reach it, turn left onto the B4235 as you leave the car park and drive a mile up the road to a small car park on the right. The bridge and pool are about 50m through the trees.

"The Launderette" is a great place for water games

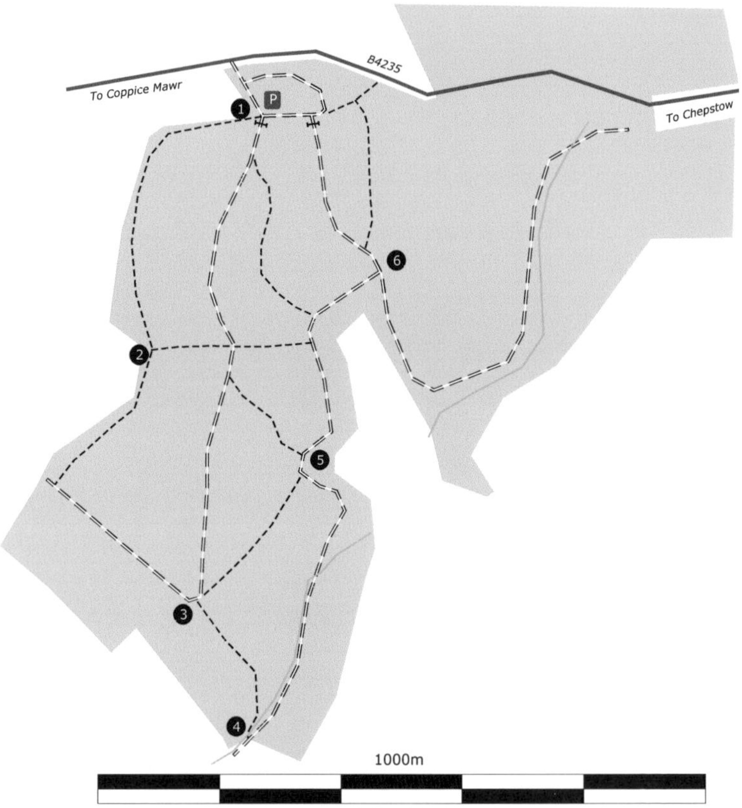

Barnetts Wood Map

Piercefield Park

Distance : 4.1km
Difficulty : Moderate

Walk Description This walk is located on the northern outskirts of Chepstow, just behind the racecourse, and is very popular with Chepstow residents. Piercefield house, now a grade II ruin, was built in about 1700 by the Wilson family from the profits of their sugar business, and extended over the next 100 years.The parkland was originally laid out in the mid 18th century and is an early example of picturesque landscaping. Many of the features and viewpoints still exist in the park.

The walk crosses the parkland past the ruins of the house, and returns along the valley rim. On the way back it passes three original features from the 18th century park: the Grotto, the Platform and the Alcove. An optional walk to the Giant's Cave passes other picturesque features. Be aware that there is sometimes a small flock of sheep in the park, but they are easily avoided.

How to get there From the racecourse roundabout on the A466 take the exit signposted for the town centre. Follow Welsh Street for 100m and turn right onto Piercefield Avenue. Park on the north side of the road beside the trees.

Directions The start of this walk is not obvious because it gets overgrown in the summer. Just opposite the entrance to Piercefield Avenue there is an earth ramp leading to a small arched gap in the wall. At the bottom of it a footpath sign points towards the arch, just beside the poop bin. This is point ❶. Go through the arch and into some woodland.

After a short distance the path joins a wide gravelled track. Follow this track through the woods to a pair of gates that open onto the parkland at point ❷. The gates can be bypassed through a kissing gate on the right. In front of you is a large open area of parkland

The Start of the Walk

that once belonged to the owners of Piercefield House.
Walking along the track, with the racecourse on your left, you'll see the distant ruins of Piercefield House across the parkland. The walk takes to to the right of the ruins. Take some time to look around and enjoy the location. On the skyline to the left you can see Chepstow Park Woods, the location of the walk in chapter 11. Off to the right you can see the woods that drop into the Wye Valley, and views across the Severn estuary into England.
Continuing along the track you'll come to fork in the paths with a small rock on your right. Take the right fork and follow the grassy path towards the ruins. Pick up the safety fence that goes along the front of the house. Pause a while and try to imagine what the house must have been like in its heyday. Continue following the safety fence through some trees and you'll come to a dog-friendly stile at point ❸.
Cross the stile, and follow the path as it slopes down rightwards onto the Wye Valley Walk. If your dog is likely to dash off down the hill you might want to put it on a lead until point ❹.
The walk turns right here, but there is an interesting diversion to the Giant's Cave and its viewpoint if you turn left. The view from the cave across the river to Wintours Leap are very attractive, and the walk visits more of Piercefield's picturesque features. Simply retrace your steps to point ❸ after visiting the cave.

The remains of Piercefield House

If you're not going to the cave, turn right along the walk towards Chepstow. As you follow the path you'll catch glimpses of the river through the trees. The river is about 100m below you and the ground is quite steep.

After a short while you'll come to the grotto on the right. The view is now overgrown, but it is easy to imagine Georgian courting couples enjoying the solitude of this spot. The Grotto is on the site of an older structure, an iron age fort. Traces of the earth rampart can sometimes be seen when the undergrowth dies back in winter.

After the Grotto the path has a short descent. This section of the path can get muddy and slippery in winter, but can be bypassed through the trees on the left. Your sure-footedness is rewarded when you reach the platform.

The platform must have been a tremendous viewpoint before the forest was established. The modern path runs above the platform, but in the trees blow the platform you can still see signs of the supporting wall for the 18th century path.

Walking on from the platform you come to the last of the original structures, the Alcove (point ❹). There is a steep drop at this point so its worth putting your dog on a lead. Unlike the Platform, the view from the Alcove is largely unchanged. The foreground is dominated by the walls of Chepstow Castle, to the left of which you can see the bottom of the old town. The M48 bridge brings the scene into the modern era. This is a lovely view on a summer evening with the sun behind you.

As you leave the Alcove the path takes you up a flight of steps. As

Chepstow from the Platform

you reach the top of the steps there is a gap in the wall to the left. This path goes to the leisure centre.
To return to point ❶ continue straight ahead along the wall. A path trends right into the woods away from the wall. This takes you back to the track between points ❶ and ❷. When you reach the track turn left and it will take you back to the start at point ❶.

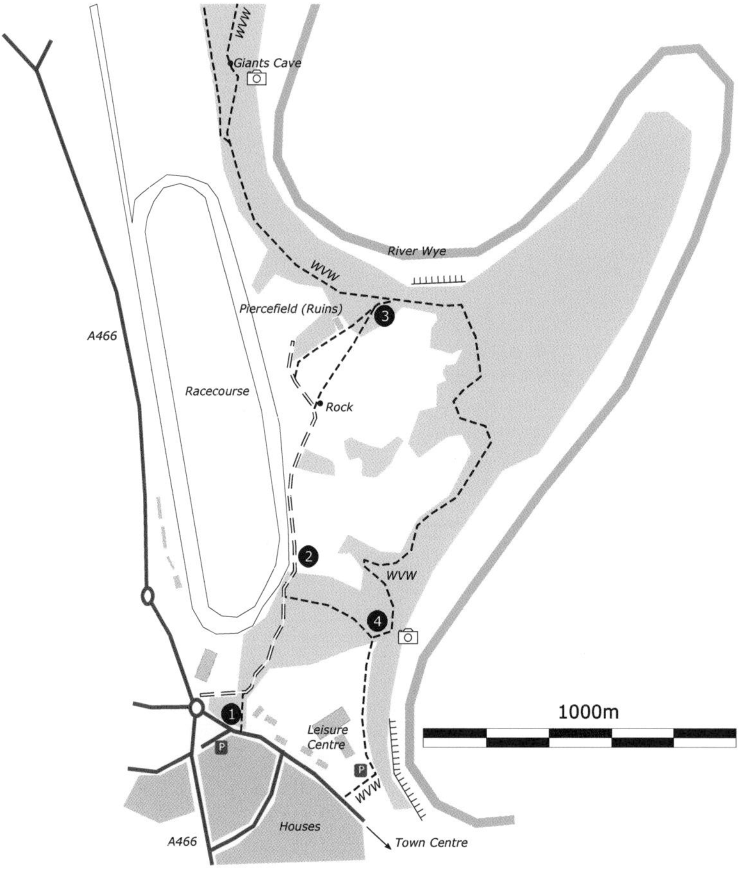

Piercefield Park Map

The Tail End

We hope that you've enjoyed the walks in this book as much as we've enjoyed writing it. You might also enjoy Holly's walks in the Forest of Dean.

If you have any comments or suggestions about this book then we'd love to hear from you. Please email your comments to holly.labrador@hotmail.com.

Printed in Great Britain
by Amazon

60069053R20043